ACKNOWLEDGEMENT

GLORY BE TO GOD ALMIGHTY

Table Of Contents

The Ultimate Guide to Setting Up Your Drop Shipping Store: Tips and Tricks for Success

Introduction:

Dropshipping has turn out to be one of the most popular on-line businesses in recent years. It is a business model that allows marketers to promote merchandise with out owning or storing stock. This way that you could begin a dropshipping enterprise with very little capital and operate it from everywhere within the global.

In this book, we are able to take you via the step-by-step system of beginning your dropshipping career. We will cover everything from locating a product area of interest, setting up your on line shop, finding suppliers, advertising and marketing your merchandise, and handling your enterprise.

Benefits of Starting a Drop Shipping Store

Before we dive into the nitty-gritty of setting up a drop shipping save, let's talk some of the blessings of this commercial enterprise version. First and important, it allows you to begin your own commercial enterprise without having to invest a number of money upfront. You don't need to worry about shopping stock or renting a warehouse. All you need is a website and a provider, and you are good to go.

Secondly, drop delivery permits you to promote a much wider variety of merchandise while not having to worry about garage space. You can listing as many merchandise as you need for your internet site while not having to fear about wherein to shop them. This way you can provide your clients a much broader variety of picks, which can in the end bring about extra sales.

Lastly, drop delivery is a exquisite manner to check the waters earlier than committing to a particular product or niche. You can effortlessly upload or remove products out of your website depending on their reputation. This manner you could experiment with distinct products and niches without having to worry about getting caught with a product that doesn't sell.

CHAPTER 1
Understanding Dropshipping

Definition of Dropshipping:

Dropshipping is a retail achievement method where a web save doesn't hold the products it sells in stock. Instead, while a store sells a product, it purchases the item from a 3rd-birthday party supplier, who then ships it immediately to the consumer. This way that the seller doesn't must take care of the product immediately, and doesn't need to fear approximately inventory control or delivery logistics.

How Dropshipping Works:

The process of dropshipping entails the subsequent steps:

1. The seller sets up an online keep and lists products from a supplier.

2. A patron orders a product from the seller's on-line shop.

Three. The supplier then orders the product from the provider and pays for it at a wholesale price.

Four. The supplier ships the product at once to the customer.

5. The seller earns a make the most of the difference among the wholesale charge and the retail rate.

Benefits and Drawbacks of Dropshipping:

Benefits:

- Low startup costs: Dropshipping doesn't require a massive initial funding or inventory control.

- Flexibility: Sellers can paintings from anywhere and might without problems upload or do away with products from their online save.

- Scalability: Dropshipping permits sellers to speedy scale their enterprise without stressful approximately inventory management or transport logistics.

Drawbacks:

- Low income margins: Since dealers are shopping merchandise at a wholesale charge, their income margins are regularly decrease than in conventional retail.

- Limited manipulate: Sellers don't have manage over the product first-rate or shipping speed, which could negatively effect the consumer enjoy.

- Competition: Dropshipping is a famous business model, because of this that there is lots of competition in many niches.

Common Misconceptions approximately Dropshipping:

- Dropshipping is a get-rich-brief scheme: Dropshipping requires hard paintings and determination to be triumphant.

- Dropshipping is easy: While it is able to have a lower barrier to access than traditional retail, dropshipping nonetheless calls for attempt and studies to achieve success.

- Dropshipping is a rip-off: While there are a few awful actors in the dropshipping enterprise, there are also many valid and successful agencies that use this model.

Chapter 2:

Finding Your Niche

Importance of Finding a Niche:

Finding a niche is vital for dropshipping fulfillment because it lets in dealers to consciousness their efforts on a specific audience and product class. This can assist dealers differentiate themselves from their opposition and construct a loyal patron base.

How to Choose a Profitable Niche:

1. Identify your ardor and interests: Choose a spot which you are enthusiastic about and feature expertise of. This will help you live stimulated and inquisitive about your commercial enterprise.

2. Research market demand: Look for niches that have high demand but low opposition. You

can use gear like Google Trends and Amazon Best Sellers to discover popular product classes.

3.   <u>Analyze competition</u>: Research your competition in your preferred area of interest to pick out their strengths and weaknesses. Look for possibilities to differentiate your self and provide precise cost on your clients.

4.   <u>Evaluate profit ability</u>: Consider the earnings margins for products in your chosen area of interest. Look for products that have a high retail charge and low provider cost.

<u>Researching Your Niche:</u>

1.   <u>Use keyword studies tools</u>: Use gear like Google Keyword Planner and Ahrens to pick out popular seek terms and topics associated with your niche.

2.   Check social media: Look for popular social media accounts and hashtags related to your niche. This allow you to become aware of trends and popular products.

3.   Read enterprise news and blogs: Stay up to date on the today's information and tendencies in your area of interest via following industry blogs and information outlets.

Understanding Your Target Audience:

1.   Identify demographics: Identify the age, gender, vicinity, and hobbies of your target audience. This will let you tailor your advertising and marketing and product services to their wishes.

2.   Conduct surveys and consciousness businesses: Ask your target audience for comments to your product offerings and marketing messages.

3. <u>Monitor client feedback</u>: Listen to your customers' feedback and use it to improve your products and consumer enjoy.

By following these steps, you could find a profitable area of interest and construct a successful dropshipping commercial enterprise.

Chapter 3:

Setting Up Your Online Store

Choosing a Platform:

When setting up your on-line save, it's crucial to pick a platform this is person-pleasant and has the features you need. Some famous platforms for dropshipping consist of Shopify, WooCommerce, and BigCommerce.

Registering Your Domain Name:

Your area name is the deal with of your internet site, so it's vital to pick one that is memorable and clean to recall. You can sign in your area name through a registrar like GoDaddy or Namecheap.

Designing Your Website:

Your website design ought to be easy to navigate and visually attractive. You can choose a premade theme or hire an internet dressmaker to create a custom layout for your internet site.

Integrating Payment Gateways:

Payment gateways assist you to method bills from clients. Some famous fee gateways for dropshipping include PayPal, Stripe, and Square. You need to pick out a payment gateway that is stable and dependable.

Creating Policies and Terms of Service:

Your internet site ought to have clean policies and phrases of provider to defend each you and your clients. This must include records on delivery, returns, refunds, and privateness guidelines.

Chapter Four:

Finding Suppliers

How to Find Suppliers:

There are several ways to find suppliers in your dropshipping commercial enterprise. You can use on-line directories like AliExpress, Wholesale Central, or SaleHoo. You also can attend exchange shows or contact producers without delay.

Evaluating Suppliers:

When evaluating providers, you need to do not forget the subsequent factors:

- Product great: Ensure that your provider gives high-quality merchandise that meet your standards.

- Pricing: Look for providers that offer aggressive pricing and affordable shipping fees.

- Shipping instances: Choose suppliers that offer fast shipping times to ensure a positive client revel in.

- Communication: Look for providers which are responsive and smooth to communicate with.

Negotiating with Suppliers:

Once you've got recognized ability suppliers, you may negotiate with them to get the first-class charge and terms. Be certain to invite about discounts for bulk orders and negotiate transport costs.

Building a Relationship with Your Suppliers:

Building an amazing relationship together with your suppliers can help you secure higher pricing and make certain a consistent supply of products. You can keep communique along with your providers to live knowledgeable about new merchandise and promotions. You also can provide feedback for your providers to help them enhance their products and services.

Chapter Five:

Marketing Your Products

Creating a Marketing Strategy:

A marketing method outlines how you'll reach and engage with your target audience. It must encompass a clean information of your target market, your precise selling proposition, and the channels you may use to reach your customers.

Utilizing Social Media:

Social media may be a effective tool for promoting your merchandise and engaging with your customers. You can use platforms like Instagram, Facebook, and Twitter to exhibit your products, run promotions, and have interaction along with your target backlinks

Search Engine Optimization (search engine marketing):

Search engine optimization involves optimizing your internet site to rank better in search engine consequences pages (SERPs). This will let you appeal to extra natural site visitors on your internet site. You can optimize your internet site with the aid of the usage of applicable key phrases, creating tremendous content material, and constructing backlinks.

Email Marketing:

Email advertising involves sending promotional emails on your subscribers. You can use email advertising to sell new products, run promotions, and construct relationships along with your clients.

Paid Advertising:

Paid advertising and marketing includes purchasing ad area on systems like Google, Facebook, and Instagram.

You can use paid marketing to reach a bigger target audience and promote your merchandise.

Chapter 6:

Managing Your Business

Managing Inventory:

Effective inventory control is vital for dropshipping fulfillment. You ought to monitor your inventory ranges and order merchandise out of your suppliers in a timely manner to avoid stockouts.

Fulfilling Orders:

When a client locations an order to your website, you have to place the order together with your provider and provide the transport info to the dealer. You need to additionally speak with the client and provide a tracking quantity once the order has been shipped.

Customer Service:

Providing tremendous customer support is vital for constructing a loyal client base. You have to respond to customer inquiries directly and provide answers to any troubles that arise.

Accounting and Bookkeeping:

Keeping correct economic records is important for coping with your commercial enterprise budget. You ought to maintain music of your earnings, charges, and earnings the usage of accounting software like QuickBooks or Xero.

Scaling Your Business:

Once your enterprise is up and strolling, you could awareness on scaling your commercial enterprise. This could involve increasing your product services, optimizing your advertising method, or investing in new era to streamline your operations.

CONCLUSION:

Starting a dropshipping business may be a lucrative and profitable profession. However, it calls for tough paintings, determination, and a willingness to research. By following the steps outlined in this manual, you'll be nicely on your manner to constructing a worthwhile dropshipping business. Remember, success comes from persistence, endurance, and a willingness to adapt to alternate.

In conclusion, putting in a drop delivery shop can be a profitable and convenient manner to begin your personal ecommerce commercial enterprise. By following the steps mentioned on this guide and imposing the recommendations and hints furnished, you may increase your chances of fulfillment inside the drop shipping enterprise. Remember to stay centered on providing exceptional customer service, staying updated with traits, and heading off not unusual mistakes. With hard work and dedication, you may construct a a success drop shipping store that generates a consistent move of income.

For Support

You can contact us using the information below

Whatsapp:+2349122404210

Email: oludareelijah14@gmail.com

Thank You For Your Patronage